AMERICAN HEROES:

STUDENTS
WHO
LEARN

Will Clark

AMERICAN HEROES: STUDENTS WHO LEARN

Copyright © 2011by Will Clark

ISBN-13: 978-1461159056
10: 1461159059

Published By
Motivation Basics
P.O. Box 6327
Diamondhead, MS 39525
228-255-5019
Will01@aol.com

For more information visit the author at:
AuthorsDen.com

CONTENTS

Goals of This Book

To help students learn how to learn by understanding the process and by accepting the idea that they have gifted abilities and success potential and are capable of wonderful achievements. However, those wonderful achievements must be earned with sincere effort and dedication to the task of learning. Society owes them nothing but opportunity to develop their success potential. Each student chooses his or her own success or failure; that choice often made from home, peer, or other cultural or natural influences and conditions.

To stress to students that they are too important to the future security of the United States to allow themselves to be less than they can be. To succeed just enough to get by and not enough to create happiness for themselves and their families is the same as failure of their potential and responsibilities. They must be proud American heroes and learn enough to protect America and understand and defend the U.S. Constitution. Evil and unpatriotic forces constantly try to destroy the principles upon which our Constitution was founded.

To help students know they must become American heroes because they are our fortress against the tyranny Thomas Jefferson warned us about. They must be aware there are many negative forces at work in America encouraging them to be followers and failures, not knowledgeable citizens and real American heroes.

QUOTE

"A nation can survive its fools, and even the ambitious. But it cannot survive treason from within. An enemy at the gates is less formidable, for he is known and carries his banner openly. But the traitor moves amongst those within the gate freely, his sly whispers rustling through all the alleys, heard in the very halls of government itself. For the traitor appears not a traitor; he speaks in accents familiar to his victims, and he wears their face and their arguments, he appeals to the baseness that lies deep in the hearts of all men. He rots the soul of a nation, he works secretly and unknown in the night to undermine the pillars of the city, he infects the body politic so that it can no longer resist. A murderer is less to fear. The traitor is the plague." Marcus Tullius Cicero, 58 B.C. Speech in the Roman Senate

What did Thomas Jefferson say should be our main purpose for education?

To be knowledgeable enough to recognize tyranny in any form. Otherwise our republic, The United States, cannot protect itself against those who would do us harm. That threat is constant. There are many who would prefer to have personal power than to serve our nation honorably.

YES, STUDENT,
YOU ARE
A NEW AMERICAN HERO

Okay, so you are a student in the fifth, sixth, seventh, or eighth grade and you wonder why school and learning stuff is so necessary. Everybody tells you it's so important, but you already know how to read, write, and count. You probably ask why you should keep studying so hard trying to learn more when you already know how to read and count.

Maybe that's true. Maybe if you can just read and count you can get by in society. Maybe you can find a job that pays someone who can just read and count. That job might be enough to let you survive and get by, or it might be enough if you always have to ask your parents or other relatives to help; to give you money when you need it to pay rent and buy food. Maybe you can just survive by just reading and counting, but is that enough to make you happy? Is that enough to be able to help your friends when they need help?

Being able to read and count is very important. Long ago it was even enough to get a good job if you knew someone who would let you try that job to prove how effective you were. Now there are so many people who can read and count and do so much more that most good jobs are reserved for them. An employer always asks, "Why should I hire someone who can barely read and count when I have so many other more qualified workers to choose from? Why should I waste my time on someone less qualified?"

7

Reading Opens Learning Doors

But, trying to learn more, and do your best, is more than just for getting a good job and having enough money to buy things you need and want. We all look forward to those things as students and even as adults. It's great to have a nice car, a pretty house, and many good friends. Now, in this current society, having a good education - learning - is becoming even more important. It's not just for helping you get things. Now, it's for helping you understand more complex and important things to protect your country. Without your country, the United States of America, being preserved in the way our original Founders intended, your children and grandchildren might never feel the freedoms under which you live, today.

One of the great founders of our country was Thomas Jefferson. Jefferson, along with others who developed our Constitution, the document designed to guide the way we have freedom and liberty in America without infringing upon other's freedom and liberty, was greatly concerned about our education system of the future. His strong proposal was that education should be guided by the principle of teaching citizens, children, how to protect themselves against individuals or groups who would use their elected positions to destroy the principles of our Constitution which guarantee freedom and free will to every American citizen. Never has our country, the America we love, been in such jeopardy that Thomas Jefferson warned us about.

As a learning student, you are now the most important citizen to help preserve the principles of our Constitution that protect our American freedom. Now, it's not enough that you just learn how to read and count. Now, you must learn to read, interpret, and understand every word and subtle meaning of our Constitution. Our Constitution and way of life as free citizens are being attacked. This attack is very sneaky and subtle. There are no bombs being dropped; there are no fire alarms ringing; and there is no one yelling, 'fire.' Our attackers are very sneaky. Their plans don't match their words. They don't yell, "charge," that they are attacking.

Those who plan to change our way of life without our approval say nice words that sound really great. They say what we are going to do for more people. They say how we will all be more equal, and how all our work will be more evenly shared. They say they will spread our wealth around to other people. They suggest that those who have more things we all hope to get, like more money, nice cars, and bigger houses, are greedy and selfish and don't care about their fellow citizens. They say nothing about those people having to educate themselves and work to earn those things.

To someone who can only read and count and have not tried to be successful, these things sound really great. It means they can have more success, all the nice things they want, without having to learn more and work hard. They can be successful by learning and working, or by just being lazy and letting our government give them more things most people work so hard to get.

This is the danger and treachery Thomas Jefferson warned us about if education just focuses on reading and counting. Education must also include enough knowledge to defend ourselves against tyranny and treachery. That knowledge means you must understand the underlying and hidden meaning of each word and phrase. People can use nice words and flowery words to make you believe they are trying to do good things for you. It's only a sneaky way to make you support them, and vote for their ideas. They will promise you anything to make you vote for them, to give them more power.

Conflict of Values

Even though our ancestors worked together to write our Constitution which now protects our freedom, they had many differing opinions during that process. They looked at the same questions and saw many different answers. Some thought it would be better to have a strong central government to make sure citizens of all the states were treated equally. They thought more control would make better democracy.

Others, including Thomas Jefferson, saw a great danger if the central government had too much power. How could citizens defend their freedoms if one central power was in control of everything? What if the leader of that central power was more focused on his own position of power than on allowing more citizens to have their individual power of self determination? What if that central leader with that much power decided to make his child the next leader of America without having elections and votes? Who could stop him?

This difference of opinion regarding a question, how to write the Constitution, is controlled by a conflict of values. Some want others to be allowed to decide their own freedom and destiny; others want to be in a position of power to give it to them. If all leaders were honorable, this would not create the problem Thomas Jefferson anticipated. Everyone could still enjoy liberty and freedom - so long as the leader allows it. The problem is that too much power corrupts the leader. That leader sees and evaluates things only from his or her one view. That view often conflicts with other people's views and needs. Eventually, that leader becomes a tyrant. Even a good tyrant restricts the free will of citizens.

When one group, one organization, or one person tries to control the actions and desires of others, that is not the way our Constitution was conceived and written. We each must be allowed to succeed in our own individual way. Others must not determine that route for us, and others should not be in a position to force us to support their success. For example, we should be allowed to go directly to an employer to ask for a job we want. We should not be required to join or ask another control group before we are allowed to ask for that job - to seek that personal success.

Many people with honorable intentions to be good workers for themselves and their employers are not allowed to do that because their future is controlled by another organization that determines their destiny.

To be able to see that burdensome handicap, you must be able to do more than read, write and count. You must learn, and have enough insight and understanding to comprehend how things are merged. In other words, if others are controlling your destiny, you will never have the right success path that will allow you to reach your highest level of happiness. In a group that controls your success, the only one who will be rewarded is the one fulfilling his goals of power and control. You will only be a controlled puppet. The leader of that group just wants more power to control you, and any others he can.

Socialism and Capitalism

To be a hero and to be someone who tries to learn more than reading, writing, and counting, there are two concepts that are very important to understand. These are the concepts of socialism and capitalism.

Our country, The United States of America, and our Constitution, were based on the concept of capitalism. This is also called the 'free enterprise' system. This is based on the idea that each person in the United States is free to decide what job or profession he or she would like to do, and how far they would like to succeed. It means that they can choose to get an education, get a job of their choice, or start a business of their own. They don't have to ask anyone's permission to make that choice, as long as that activity is legal. Capitalism is a free choice system.

Socialism is completely different. Under socialism, the government controls almost everything. Under extreme socialistic conditions, the government tells you if you can go to school, which school you will go to, if you can go to college, and what job you can have. The government assigns you to a job. Then the money you make is shared with all other workers under that system. If you are lazy and don't like to work, you still get the same pay as anyone who works hard and tries to do his or her best.

Under this system, everybody is treated the same, except for those in charge. They decide what they want and need, and they decide what you need and can have. Ordinarily, those in charge always stay in charge because they never let anyone else have that power position. Socialism means workers have no determination about how much success they will have.

Would you like to work harder than everyone else, then get the same as the others who do nothing? If you decide to do only what the others do, do you think your workplace can be successful? If all workplaces are like that, can your country, America, be successful and allow anyone else to be successful?

These are they basic differences between capitalism and socialism. Socialism is not guided or allowed by our Constitution. Your choice to be a hero will be determined by your respect for our Constitution, your love of your family and friends, and your idea to make America a better place for your children. You must now be a new American hero to protect that Constitution that protects you, your future, your happiness, and our country - our America.

Duty

Who do we usually think of when words such as: duty, honor, country, sacrifice, and dedication are used? It's common to think of people who are in the armed services, military people, since they are on the front lines often exposing their lives to bullets and bombs from dangerous enemies. Once they take an oath to defend our country, they are honor- bound to perform that duty.

Other Americans, merely by the act of not rejecting their American citizenship, are also honor-bound and historically obligated to fulfill that duty. That unspoken oath comes with their acceptance of citizenship. Of course their duty is different, since they don't bear military arms to defend America. Their duty is to contribute something to make America even better and to choose leaders who will be the best to defend America and our Constitution. To do that, they must be educated enough to get a job and to understand when politicians make false promises, or promises to do something that shows disrespect to our Constitution.

As a student, your duty is to help protect our country and make America even better. You will be a real American hero when you study and learn enough to read and write well, understand numbers, and interpret the dangers that threaten America.

Once you understand those dangers, as an America hero you will be able to make the right choices. Those right choices will allow America to still be the great land of opportunity when your children step forward to be more heroes to defend America. Those dangers will not go away. They will always be trying to destroy our freedom. There will always be someone who becomes a leader of America who will not fully support our Constitution. You must be prepared, by learning enough, to recognize them.

Thomas Jefferson will be proud of you when you are able to do this. Other loyal Americans will also respect you and be proud of you when you do your best to become a good citizen and a proud and loyal American.

The next story is true. The purpose of the story is to show that learning is not always easy, but it's always possible. It demonstrates that the secret to learning, or doing anything else well, is to begin with small steps and don't expect too much too soon. Just by taking many small steps you can do anything, even become a great learner - an American hero.

Reading Opens Learning Doors

A Basic Learning Experience

The other end of my cotton row was a long way off. Most times I couldn't even see that end because the rows curved in several places. In the Central Mississippi hill country cultivated rows were curved around the slope's contour to keep dirt from washing away during hard rains. Cotton rows followed the same curves as the heavy-duty terraces placed at certain intervals, their closeness depending on the severity of the slope. I had been down these rows many times already and, although I couldn't see the end, I knew how far it was. It was a long way, and looked forever away for a bare-foot, ten-year-old boy.

I had seen cotton rows in the flat lands of the Mississippi Delta. They were straight, but so long one couldn't see the end of those either; some as long as a mile. I wondered how one could ever get to the other end of those.

Early in the growing season rain was welcome to make the cotton seed explode, but while that happened grass and weeds usually drank first and surged well ahead of the cotton plants, selfishly trying to leave none for their later rival. At that time, in the early nineteen-fifties, herbicides were not available, especially for small-acre farmers. The only dependable herbicide was a hoe, a tool with a handle much longer than the height of most ten-year-olds. Some still exist today, most in historical museums or propped in a seldom visited corner of a hardware store. In the nineteen-fifties, and before, it was the weapon of choice to fight grass and weeds in cotton and corn fields. Special pride blossomed from those who owned one with the best shape or the sharpest edge. When I was the youngest in the field, mine was always the most dulled reject with which I had to beat grass and weeds into submission rather than cut them with a sharp edge.

Reading Opens Learning Doors

Chopping cotton was long, hard, and tedious work for a ten-year-old or one of any age. Just getting to the other end of one row was challenging. That process, seemingly simple, was more complex than could be imagined by one lacking that experience. The process could even be compared to saving a new-born baby from dangerous bullies. That new, fragile plant, only three or four inches tall, often was strangled by tenacious and hard grass and weeds. Why, then, the complicated process? Hoeing (chopping) the grass too close to the cotton plant often destroyed the fragile plant. Not hoeing close enough or deep enough left determined grass continuing its death stranglehold. It was difficult not to destroy the plant when the dirt was either too hard or too soft and flaky. Too many destroyed plants left the cotton field too sparse for a profitable yield. Too much grass created the same result, with stunted cotton plants. Sixty years later I still remember that process: leave three or four plants standing in a group, each group a little more than the width of a hoe blade apart. That allowed the removal of grass from all four sides of the plant, not just two sides.

For a profitable yield, serious decisions were required with every stroke of that hoe. Even with a perfect yield, our three-acre cotton farm was unprofitable. Only three acres were authorized for my family under the acreage allotment system at that time. My friends think I'm joking when I say I was raised on a three-acre cotton patch. Although only three acres, there was always hope for a higher acreage allotment and a better yield next year. Those anticipated better years never came for small hill farmers.

My responsibility expanded when I was fourteen. Until then my great-uncle plowed the field with a hand-held plow pulled by a horse or mule. He was a share-cropper for a larger farmer, and plowed our field during his spare time. His father, my great-grandfather, had also been a share-cropper after the end of the Civil War. At fourteen, I assumed that duty. I was surprised to learn the basic task was the same as hoeing, but the responsibilities were greater. For example, the horse or mule was a living creature who required care, concern, and nourishment. The extent of that concern was often determined by the type of plow the animal had to pull, the time of day, and the time of year.

Basic preparation of the soil was performed with a plow called a middle-buster. It was a deep running plow which threw dirt from both sides to form half a new row on both sides. A pass in the center of the next old row formed the new planting row in what had been the trail the previous planting season. A turning plow had a blade on one side forming half a middle-buster which finished forming the planting row and added more dirt volume. The sweep plow was a skimming blade angled out on both sides to cut and remove weeds and grass in the trails between the raised planted rows. A side-harrow was a springy rake-like device that loosened the soil when it became too tightly compacted near the plants.

The horse or mule required more rest when pulling the deeper running plows. They also needed more water and rest during the summer months. It wasn't uncommon for horses or mules to suffer heatstroke, and even die, if they were not cared for responsibly. While following behind that horse or mule, I always knew the animal needed more rest and water than I did. I never allowed my plow animal to be jeopardized.

Just as close attention was necessary not to destroy cotton plants when hoeing, more attention was necessary when plowing. Little things became crucial and didn't permit the luxury of a wandering mind. Running the plow too shallow created an uneven and ineffective planting bed. Running it too deep was arduous for the animal. Depth was controlled by tilting the handles. Allowing the sweep plow to wander often destroyed plants on either side. A thoughtless nudge on one of the long reins would suggest the plow animal wander into the planted row. Inattention to the plow blade often resulted in jolting to a sudden stop when hitting a stump, or stepping with bare feet onto a bed of unearthed, newly-hatched snakes. I was jolted by many hidden stumps.

Fortunately, the twisting movements of a snake bed always allowed me time to jump from that danger, since the snakes were probably more startled than I, and I was quite nimble at that young age.

Those long rows weren't any shorter while following a plow. They were still from 'one end to the other.' Even when the crop was 'laid by' those rows were as long as ever, their length still seeming endless. The term 'laid by' indicated the end to hoeing and plowing, and the crop left to finish maturing, usually about mid summer, depending upon the rain. At this time we scattered dry field peas in the laid by corn field, hoping for a bountiful side crop of field peas. Thus the name 'field peas.'

Even after the field was laid by, cotton was a special case requiring constant work, and more walks down those long rows to wage war on boll weevils. They were relentless, and destroyed the hopes, dreams, and finances of many small-acreage farmers who couldn't afford more effective equipment or more insecticide to win the battle. Vaguely, I recall an arsenic-based insecticide that was very effective but was quickly removed from the market since it was determined to be a health and environmental hazard. That was after I walked those long rows many times blowing that insecticide dust from a hand-cranked blower strapped to my chest. The apparatus had two trailing ducts that blew the dusty insecticide at the cotton boll level. Certainly, I absorbed more insecticide than did the intended targets. It was so effective that common houseflies disappeared from around our house and barn for two weeks.

Picking cotton was no less arduous, but the concept of long rows was different. If the cotton yield was sparse, the other end arrived too quickly because there wasn't enough mature cotton to pick. Either rain, boll weevils, or fertilizer quality had spoiled the yield. Picking cotton in the same row for a long time was the most desirable.

Seemingly simple, picking cotton also had many potential hazards that required close attention and care. An open cotton boll became hard with spiny points when it opened to let the cotton fibre dry in the hot summer sun. Only those most experienced could pick cotton without pricking their fingers with those sharp points. Often those pricks would result in serious infections. Snakes also cooled themselves under the shade of dense cotton plants. It wasn't unusual to see one slither away when a cool area was approached. Ordinarily, moccasins and rattlesnakes would leave early, but the copperhead was always more aggressive and reluctant to give up an area. It was more practical, however, to run instead of trying to determine the snake's species. Wasp nests were another unwelcome surprise while focusing on pulling cotton from a beautiful hand-sized, prickly cotton boll.

The horses patiently waited while the vacuum tube at the cotton gin sucked the twelve hundred pounds of cotton from the wagon. That volume usually produced a cotton bale of about eight hundred pounds, the remaining four hundred pounds being cotton seed that could be sold to the gin for resale, or returned to the wagon to save for planting the next year. Value of the bale was determined after a grader examined the quality and length of the fibre. Our farm usually produced two bales, the total value of which never recovered the costs of raising the crop. That was even considering that my time in the effort was zero value, for a period of four years.

In the summer between my sophomore and junior years of high school I finally found a real job working for someone else. I delivered groceries on a bicycle for a small grocery store in New Orleans. I don't remember the name of the store, but it was on the corner of Sycamore Street and South Carrollton Avenue.

Those months, June through August, were hot and oppressive twelve hours a day, six days a week, but that eighteen dollars a week was real money I could spend. In that job, there were only four major hazards to avoid. One was to get to my destination without spilling the groceries in the basket on front of my bike. When I did, I always had eggs in the basket. Second was to avoid the child welfare inspector. Third was not to spend all my money at the Frostop Root Beer stores trying to stay cool. Fourth was to avoid the girl, my age, who lived two houses south of the store. She indicated she wanted to be friendly, but that was something totally outside my realm of experience. I knew about cotton, not girls. When I knew she was waiting for my return, I always took the long way back to the store. I survived that summer and returned home with about thirty dollars.

During the summer between my junior and senior years, I worked for my uncle Frank in Hortense, Georgia cutting and hauling pulpwood. Although the motions were different, the process was similar to farming cotton. In cotton, the process was one row at a time. In pulpwood, it was one pine tree at a time. Looking at all the rows, or all the trees, made the task seem difficult, if not impossible. Accepting the task of processing only one row or one tree, although not pleasant at the time, allowed the concept of reasonable success to be instilled.

As with cotton farming there were many hazards to avoid, and hazards in the forest had more dangerous consequences. Our equipment consisted of three chain saws and two small pulpwood trucks.

At seventeen, I was the oldest of the three boys operating the chain saws. Although careful, I still have a large scar on my left elbow where a chain saw blade hit it from only a minor distracted moment. Fortunately for me, it tore off only a strip of skin, without any muscle or bone damage. Although becoming proficient in felling a pine tree in the intended direction, occasionally one would twist with the falling motion and move in another direction. Worse yet was the tree that wouldn't fall and instead would kick from the bottom with a sudden release.

Once the tree was felled it was trimmed then cut into four-foot segments. Even the simple process of trimming the felled tree held many hidden hazards that required total focus. Sometimes the chain saw would bounce from a springy limb. Neither was it uncommon for a half-trimmed limb to release and allow the tree to fall on an out-of-place foot. Once the trees were trimmed and cut, the five-foot pieces were loaded by hand onto the truck into a volume called a cord. If I remember correctly a cord of pulpwood was five feet high, five feet wide, and ten feet long. The truck bed was about three feet off the ground, which meant the top layer of wood was about eight feet high. The higher the layer rose, the more dangerous it became to load, by hand. Many times did I jump away to avoid a two-hundred pound piece of wood from sliding awry at the top and falling on my head. Even that simple act of stacking a cord of pulpwood required planning and care, since all the pieces were not straight and level. Those little logs had to fit together like a puzzle to be safe and stable. Inattention was an invitation to certain disaster. Even today, with all the mechanization available for workers, the forest is still a dangerous work environment.

I earned a dollar for each cord we processed. That totaled about eighteen dollars each week; three cords a day, six days a week. The fifty dollars in my pocket when I returned home to start school that fall was enough to buy a bolt-action Remington shotgun for squirrel hunting that winter. I shot one squirrel, watched it look at me as it died in agony, and never shot another. I sold that shotgun for thirty-six dollars after I graduated from high school, in 1957, to have money when I left home to join the Air Force.

Understanding goals, hazards, determination, and results from focused efforts has guided my success and happiness. I learned these common concepts apply to all positive life efforts, and it's with this background and experience that I offer them to help improve educational aspirations for those with the willingness, insight, and courage to try.

Perhaps those without gifted backgrounds or ability who refuse to allow small, natural, and positive steps guide them to the end of the row will never get there. They look at the forest, not at the tree. They look at the cotton field, not the row. They only wish for success instead of seeing, accepting, and taking those little steps necessary to lead them there. Their other option is despair and failure. Personal success, including education, is a personal choice. No one, or no society, can choose it for or force it upon another person.

Unfortunately, many choose despair and failure when they refuse to accept the positive options given to us by our Creator and our country, fought for by those who sacrificed everything to form our nation, and defended by those who, still today, give their lives in service to permit those personal choices. Success is by doing; not by hoping.

TWENTY

STUDENT STUDY SKILLS

Once a student is ready to study and understands the reason for studying, he or she must then get set to study. Getting set requires specific skills and tasks. These skills concern preparing the physical environment for effective study. They and other important study skills will be identified next.

Reading Opens Learning Doors

1

Choose a good study area

The first step to create effective study habits is to choose a good study area. Choices in the average home are usually limited to the living room, the kitchen table, a bedroom, or possibly a den.

The location should be a quiet area, such as a bedroom, a den, or study. Trying to create a quiet study area in a routinely noisy area, such as at a kitchen table, is less desirable. In a routinely noisy area, the noise will be anticipated even though it might not be present. Distractions, real or anticipated, are usually magnified for an overly curious child.

Reading Opens Learning Doors

The study area should not be so quiet and distant that the child feels isolated or cut off from other people. Although the study area should be relatively quiet, the child should be in an area where he or she may avoid a feeling of isolation.

Lighting conditions are important in the study location. Generally, indirect lighting is less tiring for reading, assuming the light is bright enough. Enough light, in proper locations, should be provided to prevent glare and shadows on or near the reading material. More than one light might be necessary. A child with tired eyes certainly can't concentrate enough to focus totally on the subject.

Adequate ventilation is also necessary in the study area to allow a student to remain alert. The volume of oxygen is reduced in a closed or unventilated area. A student will not be as alert if the oxygen flow is reduced. This often creates drowsiness and lack of full concentration, which may cause ineffective and wasted study efforts.

2

Prepare the study area

When a student goes to the study area to study, he or she should be prepared to use that time to study. That time shouldn't be wasted searching for materials to help in the study process. Many students use much of their planned study time doing things that are only indirectly associated with studying, not studying. Weak students often use the excuse of looking for things they need to do homework as procrastination to avoid that study and homework. This distraction simply prolongs the anticipated agony of real work and study.

Most items commonly used with study and homework should be located in designated areas - in the designated study area. Some of the most common items are:

Pencils	Pens	Notebook paper
Pencil sharpener	Compass	Protractor
Hole punch	Stapler	Paper clips
File folders	Rubber bands	Hi-lite markers

Reading Opens Learning Doors

Dictionary	Thesaurus	Waste basket
Erasers	Alarm clock	Large calendar
Atlas	Ruler	Calculator

Why an alarm clock in the study area? The clock should be set for the planned study time, which will be discussed later. This allows focus on studying, not checking to see how much longer to study.

Fun books, books children enjoy reading, should be in the study area. When studying becomes tiring or tedious, the child can read a fun book to regain reading concentration. Reading without concentration serves no purpose.

A comfortable desk, table, or other flat surface should also be available to write on. A student who writes on a bed, sofa, or in his or her lap often develops sloppy penmanship. This often causes a student to earn bad grades, especially if the teacher can't read that writing.

Although this is a long list, most of these items are already available in most homes. Many of them, however, are moved from place to place and often are hard to find.

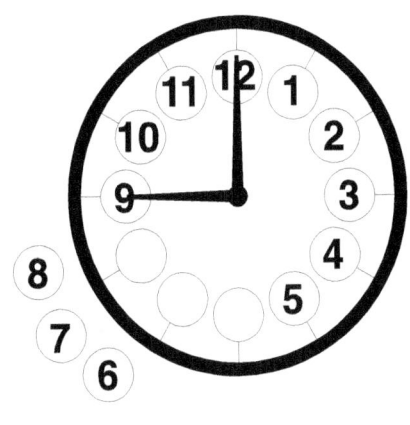

3

Set a routine study time

How often do children arrive home from school and announce, "I don't have any homework today?" Or, how often do they say, "I finished my homework at school?" Even worse, how often do they forget to do their homework?

A daily study time, at home, should be set by parents and students, regardless of the amount of homework. This creates a proactive approach to learning. It also indicates an acceptance by students and parents that the student's learning should not be determined only by the effectiveness and performance of the teacher. The child must accept responsibility for learning with the parent as a partner and guide.

Parents and students mutually should set a standard time for study. If more time is needed to complete homework, naturally that time should prevail. If the student has no homework, then he or she should use that time progressively for review, research, or improving other important skills such as reading,

The set study time should not be interpreted by the child as punishment. Talking about that time should be avoided during situations of frustration and stress between the parent and child, especially if that frustration and stress are caused by low grades. The topic should be discussed when the atmosphere is harmonious and friendly, and the conversation is focused on goals, success, and the future.

Study should not be continuous throughout the planned study time. Concentrated study time should be approximately fifteen to twenty minutes with five to ten minute rest intervals. For example, a one-hour study period would result in approximately forty-five minutes of actual study time. This schedule prevents aimless reading and drowsiness, satisfies the child's curiosity of events, and results in more effective study.

Routine and regular study time should be only part of a student's scheduled activities, since a child lives for things other than studying. The child and the parent should make sure time is also scheduled for playing, regular family fun activities, recreational activities, character building, and sleeping. These things are also important to one's development.

4

The parent must participate

Parents should be involved and part of their children's study time and study effort, especially while their children are young. Even if the parent can't help with the actual homework, or doesn't have time to solve complicated math problems, the parent must show positive interest in the study process by asking questions and offering encouragement.

Two ideas are critical to help young children learn to read and enjoy learning to read. First, parents should ask about stories read or introduced in class each day. The child should have an opportunity to show he or she can remember those stories about Dick, Jane, and Spot, or whoever happens to be popular at the time.

Secondly, the parent should listen to the young child read to allow the child to feel important. A child must feel important to develop the necessary self-esteem to succeed.

Of course the approach will be different for older students, for they have different priorities. Although a parent wouldn't ordinarily listen to an older student read, the parent must still provide the interest, encouragement and opportunity for the child's self-esteem.

Research and surveys show that students from homes that have a culture of family participation in the study process are ordinarily more successful. They make better grades, they are happier people, and they tend to be more successful after graduation from school. Some research concludes that a child's grades are more often affected by the level of parental involvement in the study process than by the level of competency of the teacher or the education system.

5

Get enough exercise

Students often fail, or fail to do their best, because they ignore physical demands and physical capacities. Student health plays a major role in student success. It's often ignored, which causes conditions that might be interpreted as lack of motivation, lack of concern, or lack of ability.

Physical exercise is considered the most important health deficiency of students. Studies indicate the brain works at higher efficiency if it has a good blood supply with plenty of oxygen. A person who doesn't exercise sufficiently deprives his or her brain, and body, of at least some needed oxygen. Authorities suggest as many as forty percent of men students and seventy percent of women students fail to get enough exercise to provide the desired oxygen flow.

Students who appear lazy might not really be lazy; they might be doing the best they can. The best they can do, however, might be limited by the physical and mental deprivation they cause themselves by being too inactive or sedentary. They might be doing their best at that time, but that might not be the best they could do if they were active and healthy.

A student should schedule a time to exercise, with the same emphasis that he or she schedules a time to study. It's not essential it be hard and strenuous. It's not even necessary exercise be scheduled as exercise. Walking briskly is sufficient exercise if it's done routinely. The student may simply accomplish chores and errands by walking instead of riding to a different location to accomplish those tasks.

Younger students, in this age of computer games, often play those games for hours instead of playing in the traditional way that creates natural exercise. This includes running, jumping, climbing, and riding bicycles. Parents should insure their young children don't ignore these normal physical activities that will help keep them healthy. Children should be taught that a well-rounded schedule is healthier than an addiction to one activity.

Reading Opens Learning Doors

6

Get enough sleep

Sleep is another important part of studying often overlooked or ignored. It's generally accepted that the average person, especially a younger person, needs at least eight hours sleep each night. Many need more than that, depending upon the person's individual personality and metabolism.

A young person, especially a student, expends much energy during a normal day. Although many students don't get enough physical exercise they still, nevertheless, expend energy. Young children play, which uses energy. Students must read, think, study, and perform in a classroom which also uses energy. Energy may be expended either mentally or physically. Energy is replenished during sleep, assuming of course the person does those other things necessary for health, such as eating the right food in the right amounts.

Sleep also allows other necessary things to happen to a person's body. It allows the body to eliminate toxins that accumulate during the day's activities. It also allows the body to repair itself in those areas where muscle and other tissues are strained or damaged. In summary, the body and the brain are allowed to rest and repair themselves.

The time for sleep must also be considered for sleep to have its best effect. Sleep is more effective if it's done at the same time - and in the same way. If a child is accustomed to going to bed at a certain time, then that time should be maintained as a regular schedule. One's body adjusts to a standard routine. If that routine changes, it takes the body some time to adjust to the new routine. If a person goes to bed at different times, his or her body might never become adjusted, calm, and comfortable. This is the body condition often referred to as 'jet lag.'

Older students should schedule their time for sleep with the same emphasis they schedule their time for study and for recreation. It's part of the over-all schedule, and just as important as any other study skill. Parents of younger children should insure their children develop a good sleep routine.

7

Don't be guided by peer pressure

Peer pressure is an influence that often discourages an otherwise good student from being a good student. Many students who have good intentions to study often are discouraged by pressure from their peers. Ordinarily, it's easy for most students to be influenced by their friends. They like their friends, they like to be around their friends, and they're comfortable with their friends. Unfortunately, negative peer pressure as well as positive peer pressure comes from one's friends. Only friends can use peer pressure. Who could be pressured by someone they didn't like into doing something they didn't want to do? Acquaintances who are disliked have no influence over a person.

How and why is peer pressure so powerful that it often replaces logic? Why is it so powerful that a person will often do something he or she knows is not the right thing to do? Peer pressure is powerful because it acts to fill basic needs that influence people.

According to motivation theories, people like to feel safe; they like to feel they belong to something important; and they like to feel respected. These likes are really needs. They need to feel safe. They need to feel they belong to something important. They need to feel respected, which creates a feeling of esteem.

Some peer pressure is positive, especially if the student is in a group with high ideals and high expectations of success. As a member of this group, a student tries to comply with the normal expectations (norms) of the group. These positive norms are respect for good grades, courtesy, understanding, and respect for each other's success.

A student who's part of a group with low ideals, low aspirations, and low self-esteem will most likely be influenced to comply with negative norms. In this negative group, a student who would mention success would be called a 'snob.' A student who attempts to make good grades would be branded a 'bookworm.' A student who tries to be respectful and courteous would be labeled a 'sissy.' A low-esteem group conditions and forces otherwise successful students to be low-achieving students.

Students with high potential and high ideals often trap themselves in negative groups that offer nothing but pressure to fail. This entrapment happens subtly and slowly. There are no bells, signs, or signals that announce: "You are now entering the influences of a low-esteem and negative group."

To remain free from the influences of a negative reference group, or low-esteem peer group, a student must make a positive and conscious effort to understand how negative peer pressure attacks a rational person, and how to avoid it. A student who's not alert might be drawn into the pits of negative peer pressure by a good friend.

The best way to avoid negative peer pressure is to develop a positive success plan and remain focused. Focusing on that goal will overcome most obstacles and distractions.

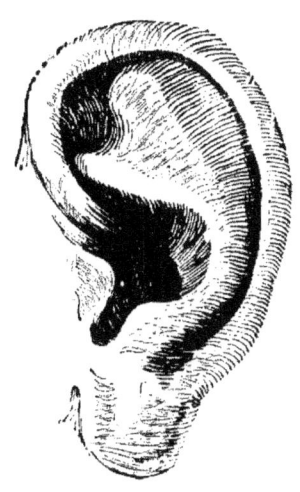

8

Learn to listen

Effective listening is a learned skill. It doesn't just happen. This is especially true in an environment where new concepts and ideas are introduced, such as in a school environment. In this environment, each word and each phrase are important to meaning and understanding.

Is listening easy? Is there no work to listening? Do you just let it happen? It's not easy; and there's lots of work to it. Let's explore some of the major problems that cause effective listening to be difficult.

Reading Opens Learning Doors

It's not unusual for someone to drift off into nice thoughts and experience daydreams. Often a person daydreams when he or she is 'listening' to someone. It would be rare if that person could listen with understanding if his or her thoughts were focused in another area. To listen with understanding - the purpose for listening - one must not only hear those spoken words, one must also actively identify and interpret each word or thought.

A person's opinion of the speaker often influences effective listening. One who listens to a friend, or to someone he or she likes, will be more open and receptive to those words and ideas. One who must listen to someone who's disliked, or someone who causes frustration, will often ignore the meaning of important words from that person. For example, it might be difficult for a student to concentrate on information given by a teacher he or she dislikes. That might cause those words to have less meaning and validity.

Another example is the relationship between the teacher and the parent. If the parent likes the teacher, the parent will be more inclined to listen to the teacher's suggestions for helping a child study. If a parent doesn't like or trust the teacher, the child's low grades will more likely be attributed to the bad teacher. The parent might regard a teacher's instructions as excuses and self-justifications.

Teacher's also have their biases. Perhaps they don't listen to a child or his or her parents because the child is regarded as an undesirable or a trouble-maker with bad parents who don't care. In many cases the child might suffer from an emotional disorder or an attention disorder, which makes positive listening difficult. Good communications must exist in all areas associated with a student for a student to gain the most from studying. The student must listen, with meaning, to learn. Parents and teachers must also really listen to help with that student's learning process.

9

Learn to take notes

Some students think they can remember what the teacher says in class. They feel they are intelligent and have good memories. Consequently, those students think it's a waste of time and effort to take notes. Students should know why it's important to take notes, how to take notes, and how to use those notes. Parents and teachers must be prepared to teach young students how to take and use notes.

Learning, especially for class work, is basically an exercise in remembering. A student must learn to remember basic facts and ideas before he or she can use those basics to form concepts and higher ideas. Remembering has a certain reinforcement schedule.

Ordinarily, something initially learned is forgotten in the first eight hours. It's forgotten, unless it has reinforcement. After only one positive reinforcement event, that fact or idea might not be forgotten for thirty days or longer. Another reinforcement event might make the memory last for several months. Of course the point is reached where additional reinforcement adds no significant value to memory.

Notes make reinforcement of memory easy and convenient. If a student takes notes during a lecture or discussion, that student doesn't have to try to remember and recall the complete lecture. If a student doesn't take notes, and the same information is not in a book, chances are the student will not remember any part of the lecture the next day unless the teacher reviews that lecture. The student must take notes, for the teacher might not repeat and review that same information.

Note-taking in class should be simple enough to allow the student to listen to the teacher while writing notes. If the student is concentrating on taking such thorough notes that he or she doesn't understand the lesson, the student might miss other important concepts and information. Notes taken during a lecture should be words or phrases that identify important information.

The student must organize his or her notes as soon as possible, preferably within a few hours. Remember, after eight hours most memory is lost if it's not reinforced. While the student is expanding those notes, he or she should also recall other information the teacher emphasized and add that to the notes. Revised notes should be complete, but they should also be condensed. A student who tries to write too many notes will use valuable time that might be used better for another subject. Revised notes should have space to add additional comments as they are remembered when the student reviews those notes.

In summary, the student should routinely review notes. The first review must be within a few hours, before the most important information is forgotten. The second review may be after a longer period. Further review depends upon how well the student remembers the material during his or her review. Once the material is learned there's no reason to over learn. That time might be needed to study another subject, or to organize notes from another class.

The student must not wait until the night before a test to review notes. The normal learning curve will not allow necessary memory reinforcement.

10

Learn to outline or hi-lite

Students often open a book, read its words, then close it without remembering what the first paragraph said. When they read the book later as a review or to study for a test, they don't review, they must read as though they had never read the material before, especially if they were daydreaming when they read it the first time.

A student who outlines or hi-lites reading material

improves his or her learning skills and makes the review phase faster, easier and simpler. Two learning concepts help make these actions more effective studying.

First, if a student prepares an outline, that student is really organizing ideas. To organize ideas one must be alert and thinking. It's difficult to let one's mind daydream if that person is really active in the reading-organizing process. It gets the person actively involved in the message instead of merely letting his or her eyes see random words.

Secondly, a student who outlines adds reinforcement to the message. Reading the material is the first action, and writing the note is the second action which is reinforcement. It's easier to remember if an idea or a fact has reinforcement.

Outlining is more effective than hi-liting or underlining in a book, although hi-liting or underlining is better than neither. Hi-liting serves the same purposes as outlining. It occupies the reader's mind and provides reinforcement, for a student will usually give some second thought to decide what to hi-lite or underline.

Outlining and hi-liting offer another great advantage. If a student becomes skilled at outlining or hi-liting, the review process becomes quicker and easier. The student doesn't have to keep reading the complete material to review and prepare for tests. He or she simply studies the condensed material, with an occasional overview of the full material to insure no important points were missed.

Although it's easier to underline and hi-lite in a book or other study material, a student must learn to outline from those study references. Some books are loaned and students aren't allowed to mark in them. In this case, outlining is the only practical answer to easy study. Outlining also allows the student to put related and similar information in the same group for better understanding.

11

Use flash cards

Using flash cards is a proven study skill, especially for younger students. Young children usually have shorter attention spans. They concentrate on something for a short time and then lose interest. Flash cards create the idea of a game, which is more fun than studying. They also fit into the short attention span of a young child. Each new flash card is a new subject to attract his or her interest.

For young children flash cards should be simple and convey only one bit of information. For example, flash cards for addition problems should have only one question and one answer on each card. Flash cards can be made on standard index cards or any other standard paper that's easy to handle. Parents should always help their young children with flash cards. Parents' involvement helps keep the child's interest focused on the importance of study time. It also helps to establish discipline in the study process.

Flash cards may also be used effectively for older students. An older student would more likely consider them note cards instead of flash cards.

Older students should have note cards for important concepts and ideas a teacher might ask on a test. They should also have note cards for standard formulas and equations that must be memorized to solve mathematical problems. Anything that pertains to a definite concept or something that must be memorized should be on a note card.

Older students should have their important note cards with them at all times. It doesn't matter if they get bent and crinkled in one's pocket. The service they provide is more important than how they look. They should be used anytime a student is waiting for something to happen or looking for something to do. Students will be surprised how much time they spend just waiting. They should use their flash/note cards during these waiting periods,

12

Improve reading skills

A student often misses key ideas and facts while studying, not because the student isn't smart, but because the student doesn't understand how to read effectively. Usually, a student who reads words slowly and carefully is concentrating on words and not thoughts and ideas those words create. Thoughts must be understood to make sense from reading. One who doesn't know how to identify those thought signals cannot make the best use of study time.

Books and other reading material have signals that tell the reader which words and thoughts are important and which are support material, definition material, or explanation material. Some signals are determined by their location in the writing and some are determined by preparatory words.

Most study and homework are from textbooks. Most textbooks are written in the common format of chapters, paragraphs, and sentences. If a student understands how these segments are arranged, he or she may learn to pick out the key points from other support information.

Book chapters are divided into paragraphs. Ordinarily, the first paragraph in each chapter tells what the chapter is about. This gives a clue to the important points in the chapter. The last paragraph often summarizes the important information in the chapter. It should reinforce the first paragraph. Before reading a chapter, the student should read and understand the first and last paragraphs. That understanding will make the chapter have more meaning.

Paragraphs usually have signals that alert readers to the main points. These are in the form of topic sentences. Topic sentences are usually first in the paragraph, but not necessarily. Often, the first sentence is an introduction to the topic sentence. Topic sentences are easy to recognize after only a little practice. A student must know they exist, however, to learn how to recognize them.

Individual sentences also have signals that say, 'Okay, here comes an important point - pay attention.' These signals are special words such as: now, therefore, however, except, greatest, important event, at this time, currently, solution, idea and theory. Many others exist and may be identified merely by looking for them.

Students often have an assignment to read only part of a chapter. When this happens the student should also read the first and last paragraphs. It reminds the student what the chapter is about, and the purpose for that reading.

A student should never read assigned homework without having a dictionary within easy reach. Children will often skip over a word they don't understand, and it might be the most important word in the reading assignment. If it's an unusual word it will most likely be a word used in a test. A student should automatically learn the definition to any word that he or she doesn't understand. If a dictionary isn't nearby, that word might remain a mystery to the student.

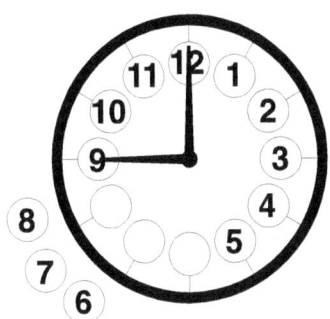

13

Use a timer while studying

If a student plans to study for an hour, he or she shouldn't spend much of that hour watching a clock to see how much longer to study. A student's mind must be focused on a subject to get the most from study time.

Five minutes of focused and concentrated study is better than an hour of studying while wondering about the time. It's difficult to interpret ideas, meanings, and concepts while reading if one wonders how much longer to study. Ordinarily, if the interest is split while reading, the reader sees only words, not ideas. The purpose for study is to remember important ideas. A timer allows one to concentrate

on his or her studies,

14

Create a good environment

The quality of a student's home environment directly affects the ability, the interest, and the motivation for a student to study and to learn. Everyone in the home is responsible for the quality of life in that home to create those conditions that allow effective study.

The student must consider himself or herself a vital part of the family. As such, the student is as responsible for conditions in the home environment as any other member of the family. Those conditions must be supportive and harmonious to allow and encourage positive actions by all members of the family; not a negative environment that creates discouragement and despair.

Parents must be the leaders in the home to set the example of a comfortable home environment. In many cases the example the parent sets is the only condition children understand. If a parent is autocratic, domineering, and unreasonable, the child will assume that's normal for a family environment. That is until the child visits families of friends who live in homes with more love and understanding.

A home environment that's ruled by loud voices, defensive justifications, threats, violence, and the unending effort to prove oneself 'right' will be focused on personality and meaningless trivia rather than on progress and meaningful goals. A child's personality and interests will be handicapped in such a negative environment.

Parents must be aware of this handicap they place on their children if they don't maintain an atmosphere in the home that will allow the student to focus on study, grades, and meaningful success. It's not unusual for the parent who screams loudest at their children for making bad grades to be the source of those bad grades by the ringing of those screams in the child's head. It's not unusual for the parent who condemns teachers most harshly for causing their children not to learn properly to prevent that learning by their harshness that distracts from that positive learning. It's just as common for some parents to blame their children for lack of interest and concern about grades when those parents never offer to help their children with homework or to prepare for a test.

A young student will have no defenses against the ravages of an unhealthy home environment. Some young students may be successful because they like their teachers, because that's simply their natural personality, or because they have good friends who make good grades.

Older students have options once they know the home

environment might contribute to their inability to focus on real and positive learning. They may try to explain the problem in the family; which might not have positive effects, for a defensive and autocratic parent would not accept the possibility that he or she could be the cause. They may find a location outside the home to study, at a routine time. The best solution, if possible, is to become part of a study group that's concerned about grades and personal success.

Teachers ordinarily recognize students who are performing at less than their reasonable ability; but the cause of that deficiency is often attributed to low motivation. Low motivation always has a cause. A negative home environment is one of those major causes. A teacher who recognizes or suspects a negative home environment as the source of a student's despair and low grades should encourage that student to find a friendly study location, perhaps the library, or to join a friendly and progressive study group.

Students and parents aren't the only people in homes who cause or create negative environments. Siblings often create that conflict and turmoil. It's the parents' duty to control those siblings to allow a child time to study without interference.

15

Choose successful friends

One's friends often determine the attitude that person will develop. Although another study skill cautioned about the influence of negative peer pressure, there's another influence that develops without pressure. That involves self-image and self-expectations. A person who thinks well of himself or herself, one who has real self-esteem, will become comfortable with other people who share those same traits.

There's an old saying, 'Birds of a feather flock together.' In applying this saying to people suggests those who regard themselves as successful, worthy, positive, and self-aware prefer to be with other people who share those same qualities. In school, these are ordinarily the students who respect themselves and other people, they have their homework prepared, they cooperate with teachers and administrators, and they participate in positive group activities.

There ordinarily are two other identifiable groups in schools. Those who flock together with negative attitudes and low self-esteem, and those who isolate themselves to remain alone, probably also from low self-esteem and insecurity. The student who remains alone may be driven to good grades to compensate for that loneliness and that feeling of insecurity. Even with good grades, however, that person remains handicapped in the success process, for a person ordinarily must know how to interact with other people to be successful.

The group that flocks together from common negative characteristics reinforces negative expectations within the group, even without peer pressure. Within that social cluster, low performance, low expectations, and low aspirations are the norms. Being successful is considered an alien condition that exists in other groups.

The positive group will say:

"When are we going to do that?"
"Do you want the homework typed or handwritten?"
"Let's get together after school and study math."
"What club or school activity do you belong to?"

The negative group will say:

"Do we really have to do that?"
"Do we have to turn in homework?"
"Let's leave school early today, or just skip."
"I stay away from all those clubs."

A positive student should become part of that positive group or, at minimum, feel that he or she is part of the positive group. This creates a feeling of normal success that makes study seem more natural.

16

Set realistic goals

Study goals should be reasonable and realistic. A student who routinely makes D and C grades shouldn't plan to make all A grades on the next report card. Although that might be possible, if the student had been a real slacker, it's not a practical approach. The student should plan to make some improvement, but not necessarily to take a giant step. The parent must be just as patient.

A student must change many things to improve his or her grades. All those things cannot be changed immediately. Study time must increase, without causing the student to become tired and weary. This includes a learning and adaptation process. Adjusting to a new study location takes time. Changing one's attitude about himself or herself takes time. One doesn't immediately change a negative self-image into a positive self-image without many 'little wins' along the way to keep that positive self-image growing. Long trips are taken with single small steps. Learning to improve grades requires that same approach. The good part, however, is that any improvement is positive improvement and reinforces the learning process.

One grade reporting cycle might not be enough to create any visible grade improvement for a student who starts with no disciplined study skills. At that time much of the focus of the student will be on the system and the method, not necessarily on effective study. There's also the possibility the next grade reporting cycle or test cycle might cover material that's unusually difficult.

Although earning good grades is important, in the beginning a student must focus more on the discipline of study than on the results of study. The student can control the discipline of study but not necessarily the results. Results will eventually occur when the student learns the process and the discipline. Ordinarily, the only difference between a C grade and a B grade is simply a little more effective study time.

Students and parents must also remember that grades may improve without that improvement being visible on a report card. For example, a grade of C might be earned with a grade average of 70 through 80. A student who improves his or her average from 70 to 80 makes a significant improvement. That should be considered one of the 'little wins' to add reinforcement and encouragement to keep improving.

Goals must be set high enough to offer a challenge and encouragement. They shouldn't be set so high they create defeat and lost aspirations. They often create worse despair if they can't be achieved.

17

Trust yourself and like yourself

Self-confidence, self-esteem, and success are things that grow together to become mutually supportive. A person who's successful will have self-confidence and self-esteem. A person who's confident will usually be successful and be proud of that success. A person who values personal pride and esteem will ordinarily be successful and confident. Since these traits accompany each other, a student may begin a good study skills program by focusing on either trait.

When first beginning to learn good study skills positive results might not begin immediately. It might take some time to learn those skills. Learning study skills is similar to learning anything else. One doesn't become a skilled ice-skater with just one lesson. That takes years. One doesn't become a professional basketball player by knowing how to bounce a basketball. That takes years of practice. One doesn't become an effective public speaker by being able to talk. That also takes knowledge and practice, including a combination of acceptable personality traits.

People become proficient in something in large part because they like themselves and they trust themselves and their dedication. A person who wants to become a professional ice-skater doesn't become discouraged and quit with the first fall, or the second, or the third. That person falls hundreds of times but never gives up. A basketball player doesn't quit when he or she misses a shot, or a thousand shots. The self-confidence keeps that person practicing one more time. A public speaker doesn't quit the first time he or she forgets a quote or becomes embarrassed before a crowd. That speaker does it one more time until it becomes natural. These winners have two special traits. They like themselves and they trust themselves.

Becoming a good student, learning good study skills, requires the same traits and dedication as becoming effective in any other facet of life. A student who likes himself or herself and who trusts himself or herself will not become discouraged and quit trying after the first fall or the first miss. That student will have the courage and dedication to try one more time.

In his book, The Power of Positive Thinking, Norman Vincent Peale advises, "When tackling a problem the number one thing is, never quit attacking it." Robert Schuller advises in his book, Possibility Thinking, "Great people are just ordinary people with an extraordinary amount of determination."

18

Don't be afraid to ask for help

Many people, including students, are afraid to ask a question or to ask for help. They don't like to ask questions for different reasons, which include:

1. They are too shy to ask.
2. They don't know how to ask the question.
3. They don't like the person they must ask.
4. They think it will make them look stupid.
5. They think the other person dislikes them.

6. They think the question isn't important.

Asking questions serves two valuable purposes. First is the obvious purpose; it creates answers to questions. If a question exists, then it's important to someone to have the answer. This is particularly valuable for a student, for one question might provide the clue to many answers.

Secondly, asking questions forces a person to interact with other people; which is itself a valuable experience. In his book, Our Troubled Selves, Allan Fromme writes, "Alone, we think less of ourselves, for sooner or later we feel rejected." He states further, "Separation from people usually becomes painful."

A student should try to find answers and solve problems by himself or herself; but that effort shouldn't become so laborious that it turns to frustration and despair. That feeling defeats the learning approach.

If possible, the student should ask the question to the teacher who teaches the subject that has the difficult question. Often, however, the student might not be comfortable talking with that teacher. In that case the student should discuss the question with another teacher, or with a student who most probably knows the answer. Most people like to be asked questions, if it's on a subject they understand. Recognizing their knowledge and ability is a compliment to them.

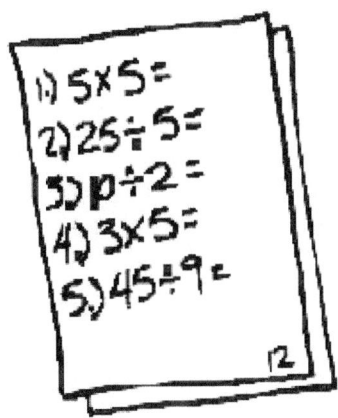

19

Learn how to take tests

A student should understand what tests are and how to take them before he or she begins to take tests. One should become test-wise in the art of testmanship. If not, that student is not prepared to do his or her best. Only a brief summary of testmanship skills will be identified here. Books are available in bookstores and libraries that give more in-depth details. Key points to taking tests include:

Review test material before the test. If the student has developed good study skills, most information will already have been learned. A review before the test, however, is necessary to test the student's memory and to reinforce important specific facts. Pay close attention to topic sentences in the basic reading material, and compare those to notes, outlines, and flash cards.

Get enough rest and sleep the night before the test. A tired mind and body are less likely to allow information to be recalled. Some tests, themselves, are physically and mentally tiring.

Understand the instructions. In the lower grades these instructions will normally be given orally by the teacher. In the higher grades, the instructions are often written at the beginning of the test. In either case, those instructions must be understood to insure questions are answered in the right manner and order, and not in reverse. Understanding the testing process is as important as knowing the answers.

Know how much time is allowed for the test. Scan through the test material to see how much time may be allowed for each section, or part. Will more time be needed for essay questions, or does the test require only choice answers?

Stay alert to key words in the test. For example, true-false tests often give clues to answers by words such as always, never, all and none. If you must guess for a true-false answer, the answer should be your strongest first impression, or 'false.'

Answer the easy questions first. This serves two purposes. First, the student knows how much time he or she has left to consider the difficult questions. Easy questions will not be left unanswered if there's not enough time to complete the test. Secondly, answering the easy questions first often provides information or clues to answer the more difficult questions. Work on the more difficult questions next. Don't use too much time thinking about the same question, unless it's the last question.

Understand the different types of tests. These include:

Reading Opens Learning Doors

* True-false
* Multiple choice
* Matching
* Fill in the blanks
* Essay

Each type of test has its special character that must be learned. As stated above, true-false tests have exclusionary words that suggest a false answer. Multiple choice questions usually have two answers that are clearly wrong. Matching questions usually have the same number of questions as answers. If one doesn't fit at the end, then one or more of the answered questions must be wrong. A fill in the blank question might give clues from other questions. Essay questions usually ask the student to inform, describe, explain or justify. The student must know the different meanings of these words. Books are available in libraries and bookstores that explain these different tests in more detail.

20

Reward yourself

Good things should be reinforced to make them happen again. This is a process called positive reinforcement. Although positive reinforcement is normally used incorrectly and abused, it should be used to enhance learning skills.

Positive reinforcement often is attempted by parents who promise to pay their children money for making good grades. This system seldom works because the money is a promise and becomes an indebtedness if the child improves his or her grades. It's not a reinforcing reward. For effective reinforcement the reward should be given by the parent, or teacher, after the good performance, without specifically applying that reward to that performance. The child must be allowed to make that association by himself or herself. That association of action and results, not the promise of a reward, creates the reinforcement.

On the other hand, the child should openly celebrate

and reward himself or herself for hard work and sincere efforts. If the student is an older child, perhaps he or she should treat himself or herself to a special movie, a party, or an extra large banana split. For the younger child, perhaps a trip to the zoo or a nearby fishing hole would be appropriate.

In any event, the reward should be based on hard work, effort, and sincerity, not necessarily grades. Good grades are only the result of that effort. If a child works hard to learn good study skills and doesn't make better grades on the next test, that effort should still be rewarded. Good grades will eventually occur if the student doesn't become handicapped by disappointment and despair.

The Success Story Continues

Okay, just for those of you who might like to write stories, after you learn to read and write well, this is an example of writing in person. The first part of the story was written in first person. That means using the word 'I.' The continuing part will be in third person. That means 'he' or 'she.' It's still my true story. I just don't like to use the word 'I' too much.

The story at the beginning of the book continues here to demonstrate that it doesn't matter where you come from, how wealthy or poor your family is, or what your handicaps are, if you want to be successful you can. You just have to decide to do it - then take many little steps to do it. Of course, there will be many heartaches and disappointments along the way. No matter how hard, it's what happens at the end of the story that really counts.

******

Born into total poverty, this child was destined to fail in life's economic struggle. His father was an alcoholic who abandoned the family when the child was four years old. His mother never graduated from grammar school, and had no career skills other than manual labor. The place was the red clay hills in Central Mississippi. The year was 1943, at the height of World War Two when basic necessities were scarce, especially for the poorest people.

Fortunately, or unfortunately as the case may be, women were suddenly in demand for hard backbreaking jobs that previously had been available only for men. Most young men were in jobs contributing directly to the war effort, so women were welcomed into the civilian workforce to fulfill those worker requirements. The mother, too proud to accept welfare assistance, moved to Pascagoula, Mississippi, to become a welder at the Ingalls Shipbuilding Company.

Their home in Pascagoula was a thirty-foot house trailer that was part of a temporary trailer compound located on Mantou Street. Bathroom facilities were located in the center of the compound. The first movie the child saw was from an outside projector flashing onto a bed sheet hung from the common bathroom building. It was a western, starring Lash Larue. The first time he heard Rudolph The Red-Nosed Reindeer, by Gene Autry, was in a little café on the corner of Mantou Street and Ingalls Boulevard. They survived: the mother, the four-year-old child, and a two-year-old brother.

When the war ended, in 1945, they migrated back to the red clay hills in central Mississippi. For several months the family lived in a three-room shack. Old newspaper from trash bins was a valuable resource there, for it was used as insulation to keep the winter wind from blowing through the gaps in the unpainted and unfinished oak boards on the outside of the framed structure. There were no inside walls or inside insulation. The shack was heated by a small pot-belly, wood-burning heater in the central room and a wood-burning stove in the kitchen. That shack collapsed two years after the family moved to another location.

The mother started working at a shirt factory for minimum wage. She quickly gained a reputation as a hard-working, dedicated, and totally honest person. Although her pay was only seventy-five cents an hour, the local bank loaned her three thousand dollars to buy a ten-acre farm that had an old house on it. The house was in barely livable condition, but it was a home and it would be repaired to be a real home. The mother wanted her two children to have a permanent and stable home so they could be educated in a secure environment. The child was now six years old and, as any normal six-year old, was excited about starting school.

This home was also heated by a wood-burning stove

and a fireplace. The out-house was really outside, fifty yards behind the house. Lighting was from kerosene lamps and candles, for there was no electricity. Water was drawn with a rope and pulley from a fifty-foot deep well. Frequently, during the summer months, salt was thrown into the well to kill mosquito larvae, locally called wiggle-tails.

The farm, ten acres of scrub land, was gully-washed and greatly endowed with an innocent looking yellow-flowering plant called a bitterweed. The farm cow, Bossy, had a constant diet of those weeds, along with the few good bites of grass she could find.

Breakfast for the family was a mixture of butter and molasses stirred together, and eaten by dipping homemade sopping biscuits. Lunch and supper for the family was usually cornbread crumbled into a glass of milk and eaten with a spoon. The milk was bitter from the weeds Bossy ate. The cornbread often had large husks, not sifted out at the local grist mill. Bossy wore out and died eight years later.

The family had a special treat on most Friday nights. It was either fried chicken or bologna sandwiches. Sometimes they even had a bag of Oreo cookies or a box of vanilla wafers.

First grade was so exciting for that six-year-old. There were new boys and girls to play with. The exuberance and anticipation of learning to add and subtract, to read real words, to tell time from a clock, and to learn about the sun, the moon, and dinosaurs, were almost overwhelming. He was awed by the fantastic new and tremendous world. Glowing with excitement he could hardly wait for morning to start each school day.

A whole new world evolved for the boy during the first three school years. Not only did he learn reading, writing, and arithmetic, he also began to understand the reality of the differences between economic and social classes. He discovered questions, such as: Why am I the only one with holes in the knees of my pants? Why do I have a peanut butter sandwich for lunch, everyday, while most of the other kids eat in the lunchroom? The answer was that meals in the lunchroom were not free. They were fifteen cents a day, or seventy-five cents a week. His mother couldn't afford to pay the fifteen cents.

When he was in the third grade the world crushed down upon him even further. He realized he could not talk and communicate like everyone else; he was a stutterer. He was totally devastated, constantly embarrassed, and had no place to hide. Ridicule, embarrassment, terror, and panic were everywhere. The harder he tried not to stutter, the worse his handicap became. It dominated every event and action of his life.

His teenage years were a constant series of panics and withdrawals. Class recitals and verbal questions from teachers made his heart rush to his throat, and caused his clothes to become soaked with perspiration. Usually, he had to decide between the choices of looking stupid by saying he didn't know the answer to the question, or of looking ridiculous by trying to give an answer to the question. He knew he could never get the right words from his mouth. He usually chose to look stupid by responding, "I don't know," to those classroom questions.

He enjoyed being around people, especially small groups. He knew individuals in small groups were usually considerate of the other people's feelings and wouldn't laugh and ridicule as would people in larger groups. He avoided large groups whenever possible. On those occasions when it was impossible to avoid being part of a large group, he was a non-participant. He had learned that a hidden compelling force existed in large groups that made people, even close friends, do or say harsh things they would never do or say on a closer personal level. Although he didn't know the name of that force, he had identified the peer pressure monster at an early age.

The most tragic event happened when he was fifteen. His closest friend, a friend for nine years, didn't invite him to his birthday party. It was inconceivable. There were tears and disbelief. He tried to imagine that his friend had forgot to invite him. He tried to imagine that his friend assumed that he knew he was invited. He wondered if he should ask - but he knew he wasn't invited, and he knew why.

The withdrawal became deeper. Surprisingly, to himself, the withdrawal was not from a feeling of anger or a sense of rejection. He realized the withdrawal from his friendships was to protect his friends from the embarrassment of associating with or being in the uncomfortable environment of a severe stutterer. Each stuttering occurrence was tense, embarrassing, and humiliating for everyone present.

Stuttering is a special problem, for it happens unexpectedly and doesn't permit listeners time to consider how to react. There's no way for a stutterer or the listener to find a mutually comfortable reaction when stuttering occurs, even when it's anticipated. He realized these were difficult times for his teenage friends, anyway, since these were the difficult years, so he often avoided close friendships and associations. His feeling was that his problem was a personal one. He would either overcome it by himself, or suffer the consequences by himself.

He got a summer job when he was seventeen. His uncle hired him to cut pulpwood. Pulpwood is from pine logs, cut into segments, measured by the cord, and used to make paper products. He worked twelve hours a day, six days a week. He was paid a dollar a cord, and usually earned twenty-five to thirty-five dollars a week. He returned to his last year of high school understanding the value of getting his high school diploma.

He had two significant high points during his last year in high school. First, he realized his intelligence level was average. He learned that if he studied he could improve his grades. He graduated with a grade exactly in the middle of his class grades. Secondly, he finally got a date with a girl. He took her to the movie, had popcorn and a coke, and took her home. It was excitement beyond imagination. He had become a normal person.

He graduated from high school in 1957, the first in his extended family to reach that goal. Finally, he had made it. Two things had kept him going to school and facing each humiliating and embarrassing moment until graduation. One was the unwavering encouragement his mother gave him about the importance of a high school diploma. The other was the idea that he could face the embarrassment and emotional trauma of being a stutterer, but the idea of being a quitter would have been intolerable. Pride and desire were too strong to tolerate quitting. He knew the goal was always to get to the end of the row.

The first giant step had been taken; he had earned a high school diploma like other normal people. Now, the next step in real life was ahead. He must venture into the real world and get a job. He wondered how he could do that, when usually he couldn't even ask a complete question or carry on a regular conversation. Even worse, saying his own name was the most difficult task. He realized one must introduce himself or herself when asking for a job, or for an application for a job.

As a simple solution to that problem he decided to join the U.S. Air Force. He knew there would be no job interview to join the Air Force. One became an applicant for the military service merely by walking into the recruiting office. It was almost that simple, since recruiters were that anxious to have another volunteer. Four days after he graduated from high school he was in basic training at Lackland Air Force Base in San Antonio, Texas.

Basic training was relatively easy, and lasted only eight weeks. Only a little interpersonal communication was required, because most training activities and events were done in group formations, where individuals were generally obscure. Little verbal communication was required, other than, "Present, Yes sir, and No sir." Even slurring those easy words was accepted as military jargon. He remained at Lackland Air Force Base another twelve weeks to complete

Basic Hospital Corpsman School. Then he was transferred to the Great Lakes Naval Training Center, in North Chicago, Illinois, to complete sixteen more weeks of advanced Hospital Corpsman School.

A whole new world had opened for this young man. The military training had already instilled several key success concepts in him. Most important were the concepts of goal orientation, personal initiative, and confidence. During the sixteen weeks of hospital school at Great Lakes Naval Training Center he completed the course as an honor graduate while he also completed tests which earned college credits. For being an honor graduate he was allowed to select his next assignment location. He chose to return to Mississippi, at Keesler Air Force Base, in Biloxi.

Real life returned during his job placement interview at the Keesler hospital. Since he still had great difficulty talking, he and the job placement counselor agreed he should be assigned to a job with only minimum verbal requirements. He was assigned to Central Supply, at that time the least desirable and dirtiest job in the hospital. This was before the common use of disposable hospital supplies, such as rubber gloves, hypodermic needles, syringes, and containers. His job was to collect used and dirty items from the hospital wards and clinics, wash them by hand, then sterilize them. The daily workload usually included 500 pairs of rubber gloves, 1000 hypodermic needles and syringes, and 100 or more basins and pans, all which contained ordinary hospital refuse and contamination. He was assigned to that job his entire time at the Keesler hospital, over five years.

He never complained about the hazardous health conditions of the job. Neither did he complain about relative rank status of the job although there were people of lesser military rank assigned to better jobs. He faced the job using the concepts of goal orientation and confidence. He devoted himself to be the best he could be from all aspects. He wanted to clean more dirty used rubber gloves than anyone else could. He would clean and sharpen more dirty hypodermic needles than anyone else could. He would also clean more syringes, basins, and pans than anyone else. Then he would ask, "What else needs to be done?"

He completed another year of college by challenge tests. Then he started evening college courses, beginning with the course he feared most: Speech 101. He believed that one day he would be justly recognized for his work and self-development goals. Eventually, he was. Three years later a doctor in the audiology department asked if he would like to attend a speech training program to help correct his stuttering problem. The therapy was a six week course at the Forest Glen Speech and Audiology Center, in Maryland.

Not only was another whole new world opened for this young man, two strong guiding principles were also reinforced. Those were: If something is worth having, then you must work for it; and, never let yourself make yourself a loser.

Speech therapy was not an instant cure, nor was it expected to be. Speech therapy for adult stutterers rarely is a total cure. This young man, however, was trained to accept the problem as one that could be handled with the proper mind set, and practice, over a long period of time. There was hope, there was a plan, there was enlightened confidence, and there was steadfast determination.

He went back to real life after completing therapy in an artificial setting that made stuttering seem less abnormal. Now, he had a wife and a young son to support and he knew he couldn't just keep working along, waiting for something to happen. Everything he had achieved so far had occurred by deliberately planning and striving for it. Nothing positive had just randomly happened, simply because he happened to be there. All the positive results had been from positive actions. A good work ethic had not just happened; the college credits had not just happened; the school honor graduate award had not just happened; and the night college courses and other correspondence courses had not just happened. They had resulted from deliberate action that had required much personal determination and effort.

Would these principles help advance his career and his economic status to support a family? So far there had been only personal achievements with no tangible or economic rewards. Let's find the answer to the economic question as his true story continues.

It was now 1960, and he was 21 years old. He had just been promoted to airman second class, which raised his monthly pay from $86 to $99. He also received $50 for family housing, which made his total monthly income $149. The outlook for promotions during that time was not good, either. Under conditions that existed at that time, low demand for the military, he knew the next promotion would take two or three more years, and promotion to sergeant no earlier than five to seven years. Should he just wait for those events to take place? He knew the answer was - absolutely not!

Experience had taught him that just to wait for good things to happen would be to wait for deterioration and failure. The only way to advance or to make progress was to do something; anything. And he did. His next goal was to complete the biggest project he visualized at that time, to pass the Air Force officers qualification test for Officer Candidate School (OCS.) Of course, he knew it would be impossible to get accepted for that school since he was a marginal student from Mississippi - who stuttered. But, just to pass that qualifying test, passed by so few, would make his qualifications more visible when he was eligible for promotion to sergeant.

The test was a day long battery of aptitude, general knowledge, and military-specific subjects. He passed the first half, graded at noon-time, which permitted him to take the second half in the afternoon. He failed that part. Although disappointed, he knew this was no great tragedy. He was elated. He had done better than most people who had ever taken the test. Furthermore, he now knew the nature and focus of the test and how to prepare for it.

During the year required to retake the test, he prepared

to accomplish that goal. He studied general information almanacs, aptitude test preparation guides, English refresher courses, map reading, aerial photography, and aircraft orientation courses. After that year of concentrated preparation he took the test again.

This time tragedy did strike. He failed the first half of the test. He was still an airman second class, and normal promotions looked further away. Although he was disappointed, he looked at his alternatives for career advancement, and again reached the same conclusion: pass that test!

Another year to wait for the test, but also another year to prepare for it: more reading, more studying, more night school, and more correspondence courses. It also required more patience from his wife to accept his dogged determination.

He was prepared again to take that test. It was the third time, after two years of focused effort. Now, however, there was a new obstacle. This was the last test cycle; his last chance. Officer Candidate School was being eliminated to be replaced by a different course, Officer Training School, which required a college degree. Had he studied enough? What was his confidence level? Was he emotionally ready? Was he good enough to pass that test, reserved for only the most qualified? This was not a guessing game or a luck test. Wrong answers on the test were not harmless. They were subtracted from the correct answers. On the positive side, though, he knew he had everything to gain, and nothing to lose. Even if he failed that test, he knew his knowledge, abilities, and perspectives had been enhanced by striving for that important goal.

The test monitor said, "Time." Pencils were placed on the desks and test booklets were passed forward. The test monitor then announced that test scores would be published at 12:30, after lunch. Applicants eligible to take the second half of the test would be notified then; in one hour. Lunch lasted an eternity.

The second half of the test passed quickly. To complete

the test there wasn't enough time to read each question carefully and double check each answer. There was only enough time to read a question, make a mark, then move quickly to the next question. He floated into an imaginary dream world when the test monitor said, "You passed!"

What a relief! What a dream come true! He had planned it, he had worked and struggled for it, and he knew he had done it himself. No one had simply offered him that success and that feeling of accomplishment on a silver platter. He realized what he needed to do, and he just worked hard enough to do it. He knew that his long-term work record plus the reputation of having passed that test would enhance his possibilities for future promotions.

Soon afterward, he was promoted to a third stripe and sent to a non-commissioned officer (NCO) preparatory school. This month-long course was designed to train airmen for NCO responsibilities. While at that school his regular squadron personnel clerk notified him by telephone that he was not selected for the OCS class. This was not surprising, for he knew he wouldn't be selected for OCS. His goal for taking the test was to help him advance through the NCO ranks.

A day later he received the formal letter that made the announcement. It stated: You were not selected for the OCS class starting October, 1962. The quota for that class has already been filled. You have been selected for the following class, beginning in January, 1963. That was the last class of Air Force Officer Candidate School.

While trying to locate the school, on Lackland Air Force Base, in Texas, he visited the information center. The clerk there told him that he, "Would never make it through OCS, for the demands are too high for someone who couldn't talk right."

The six months at OCS, January through June, 1963, was a daily routine of panic and frustration. The course consisted of six hours, daily, of academic classroom subjects in management, communications, military concepts, economics and political geography. The remainder of each day was filled with training usually associated with military activities. This included marching drills, clean-up details, drum and bugle corp practice, and disciplinary fun-and-games by the upper class. These were students in the class that started in October, 1962. They conducted the training other than academics. Study for academic classes was usually after lights out, under bed covers, with a flashlight.

He was surprised he survived. He was commissioned a second lieutenant in the U.S. Air Force, June 21, 1963. His wife shared his pride and accomplishment: she pinned the first gold bar insignia onto his collar.

The planning and perseverance rewarded him economically, as well as emotionally. His pay more than doubled in only six months. In December, 1962, his monthly pay was $148. When he was promoted to second lieutenant his pay rose to $335. Combined with the family allowance, his total pay was a little more than $500.

Planning, perseverance, and effort had helped him reach the goal of advancing his career even beyond his expectations. Was this it? Was this the ultimate goal of his career? Of course not. It was only the exciting beginning of new goals guided by higher aspirations. He had learned and reinforced the concept of the power of purposeful planning. He knew that unwavering, goal-directed efforts would produce positive results. He knew it was his responsibility to determine what his future should be. It was his responsibility to plan how to reach those goals. It was also his personal responsibility to make those things happen. He knew he couldn't wait for the silver platter of success handouts.

He was twenty-four years old and had been in the Air Force six years. To retire from the Air Force as an officer, in fourteen more years, he knew he must reach the grade of major. Otherwise, he might be reduced to his prior enlisted grade. He also knew that to be competitive for officer promotions he must have a college degree. He had another clear and definite goal; to get that degree.

Japan was his first duty assignment as an officer. There, he completed four on-base college courses: Economics, Philosophy, Conversational Japanese, and English Literature. He was in Japan two years, then was transferred to Saigon, Vietnam.

He was awarded the Air Force Commendation Medal for his service in Japan. He had been promoted to first lieutenant before he transferred, and he was promoted to captain while he was in Vietnam. No courses were available, nor was there time to take college courses, during his year there. He was awarded the Bronze Star for his service in Vietnam.

He returned to the United States, in 1966, and was assigned to Shaw Air Force Base, in Sumter, South Carolina. Shaw AFB had an active base education center, where a counselor advised him that if he completed twelve more semester hours he would be eligible for Operation Bootstrap. Bootstrap was a program in which the Air Force, and other military services, assigned its members to a college or university to complete the last thirty semester hours required for a degree.

He completed those twelve hours in one month by taking challenge tests: two in economics and two in accounting. Then he completed the last thirty hours at the University of Nebraska at Omaha, in December, 1971, to earn his degree.

In 1972, he also completed another Air Force program, Air Command and Staff College, by correspondence. He was awarded the Meritorious Service Medal for accomplishments during his six years at Shaw AFB.

He was transferred to Ankara, Turkey, in 1973. There, he entered a new life phase. Instead of being a student, he became a teacher. Instead of withdrawing from public speaking, he taught college courses so military personnel assigned there could continue their college work. He taught four semesters of real estate classes, which were on-base extension courses from the City Colleges of Chicago. These were the only college courses available for students at that time. He had completed a practical real estate course while he was assigned to Shaw AFB, and had taken an academic real estate course, and related courses, while attending the University of Nebraska.

He was promoted to major in the spring of 1974, while still in Turkey. For his performance during that assignment he was also awarded another Meritorious Service Medal (an Oak Leaf added to the first medal.)

In July, 1975, he was transferred to the defense depot at Tracy, California. He had only two more years until he could retire from the Air Force, so it was time to set new goals for a new career. He thought the real estate career offered possibilities, since he had studied and taught real estate for the past four years. Therefore, his new short-term goal was to pass the California real estate broker examination.

There were more requirements to take that test. His college degree substituted for the required sales experience, however there were six other college level courses required to qualify for the examination. He completed the required courses by correspondence and challenge tests within three months and got his California real estate broker's license in December, 1977.

In February, 1978, he requested to retire from the Air Force. Two weeks later he received a letter from the Air Force offering to send him to a university for a master's degree. What a difficult decision he faced: to remain in the Air Force, almost guaranteed of career advancements and promotions, or to retire from the Air Force and start a new career at the age of thirty-nine. He chose to start the new career. Why? Because of new challenges.

He retired from the Air Force in April, 1978. During the retirement ceremony he received the Joint Services Commendation Medal for his duty performance at the Defense Depot Tracy.

Were his productive years over? Absolutely not. They had only begun. Although he was not aware of it at that time, his Air Force career was only a learning experience preparing him to become a more positive and contributing part of society.

After his military career he completed another ten-year career in civilian industry. That ten years helped him reconcile concepts and assimilate ideas regarding success and motivation. He learned that the same fundamental success principles apply, regardless of the environment. Whether military or civilian, to be successful one must identify a specific goal then actively strive to reach it.

A successful person doesn't just wait for success to arrive - to come knocking on the door. It never does. It must be earned by getting to the end of each row, one row at a time, no matter how long the rows are. The author wrote this book just for you to help you learn how to get to the end of that row - to be the success you want to be and can be.

Never give up. Always get to the end of the row, no matter how many attempts it takes to get there. Always continue to be an American Hero, and respect and protect our United States Constitution. Why is it important that you must be a hero? Because other people might be too afraid, or too lazy.

Conclusion

Making good grades in school represents a combination of feelings, aspirations, pressures, and effort. If good grades are a student's goal and the student makes good grades then the student is successful. He or she has accomplished a goal, which is the clear and simple definition of success.

If the student's goal is to graduate from high school, then he or she has accomplished a short-term goal to achieve that long-term goal. If the student's long-term goal is to be successful in life, then the student has set a success pattern by making good grades and by graduating from high school.

Good academic grades give children much more than merely good grades they can show to their parents and other relatives. Good grades also give students pride, esteem, a feeling of higher belonging, and the attitude that success is a natural event. A child who doesn't make good grades has a general success handicap if he or she doesn't have these traits.

Although a student has the basic tool for learning, intelligence, that tool must be influenced and guided properly and positively by teachers and parents. Learning is a team effort, especially during the early years when a child is learning how to learn. Once the child is old enough to read effectively and knows how to learn, the learning process then becomes habit and motivation.

A child's habits and motivations are most influenced by the child's culture. If the child's home life and friends exemplify failure, despair, laziness, carelessness, weak values, and lack of accepting personal responsibility, the child will be disadvantaged to achieve success. Grades signify only one part of that success attitude.

Parents must set examples of courtesy, caring, responsibility, honesty, respect, and success if they want their children to understand those qualities.

Work, attitude, success, and happiness are qualities and results that go hand-in-hand. Perhaps this concept was explained best by an anonymous Irishman, as reported in Robert Schuller's book, Possibility Thinking. He stated:

"Take time for work, it is the price of success.
Take time to read, it is the foundation of wisdom.
Take time to be friendly, it is the road to happiness.
Take time to laugh, it is the music of the soul."

Even within an atmosphere of failure and despair, guided and perpetuated by personal ambitions, cowardice, or ignorance of many politicians and other senior education planners, parents can still help guide their children to success. Those students endowed with good academic skills must be allowed to reach their highest potential. Just as important, students less endowed with academic interest or prowess must not be tossed aside and have their great potential destroyed by elitists' education programs. They must be guided and assisted to achieve the maximum of their potential without destroying their positive dreams and success. Every child is destined for success in some form or avenue, and that success route is not always determined by grades. Their dreams must not be destroyed by forcing them to drop out of school because their interests are elsewhere.

Education must be redesigned to allow success avenues for all children, not just those who are academically, culturally, or socially gifted. Now, our education system is designed backwards: the purpose fits the plan, rather than the plan fitting the purpose for education. This condition is made worse since the purpose for education has not been specified by those creating the plan. The present education plan forces at least a third of our children to drop out. The failure of our country might well result more from the drop-out problem than the grade problem.

Weak grades do not create criminals and perpetual welfare cases. Currently, the cost to house criminals is greater than the cost of education. How great would be the goal of using that money now wasted to incarcerate criminals to support the motivation needs of students who now lack hope and positive dreams.

As a final thought, with the idea of trying to help sustain our great democratic society, perhaps we should heed the warnings of Thomas Jefferson more seriously. Should we compare his warning with the history of Ancient Greeks who were first to experiment with a form of pure democracy? That experiment failed when conditions evolved similar to evolutions in our democratic society, especially pertaining to welfare reform and education planning.

Are we not, today, seeing the less inspired, the less motivated, and the less successful gaining a greater voice in political decision making. Are we not, today, watching as business leaders who create jobs and more opportunity for individuals' success be denounced and vilified by those whose jealousy and lack of personal achievement distort their interpretation and vision of success?

Are we not, today, watching as the growing masses of less inspired and less motivated have a stronger voice in the call for equal distribution of wealth? Are not many political leaders, today, heeding that voice for personal gain and personal power?

How far do we have to go while we tax the wealthy more to give more to the less-inspired before we move over the dangerous precipice of socialism. Is socially engineering a standard and mediocre education system one of those major steps toward that precipice?

We must never forget that individual success,

prosperity, and happiness are earned. They are rewards from personal efforts to be educated and to contribute to our society. They are not things given freely off some silver platter of economic equality. Perhaps one who does not try to earn success rewards would not really understand or appreciate them anyway if they were accepted off that silver platter.

STAY POSITIVE
KEEP A FIRM RESOLVE

Is learning easy? Of course not. If it were easy then it wouldn't be called 'learning.' It would be called something like 'absorbing.' It would be like letting water just soak into your brain.

To really learn, you must want to learn - and understand the reasons for learning. There are three important reasons for you to learn.

First, you must learn, to allow yourself to be happy. One who feels he or she is less than he or she can be can never be happy. To be happy, you must feel that you have accomplished something positive. Happiness is life's greatest gift.

Second, you must learn so you can be successful. A whole book could be written to explain the definition of success, but we won't try to do that here. Let's just keep it simple and say that success is being able to earn enough money so you will not be a burden to other people - so you won't have to get part of their success to survive. A higher success is even accomplishing enough of your goals that you can even have enough left over to share with others. Sharing with others is the highest form of success and happiness.

Third, you must learn so you can be a brave and

positive person, a great citizen, to defend our country, the United States of America. There are many people, even leaders at the highest levels, who want to change America, to destroy the principles and freedoms upon which our ancestors fought and died to create for us. You must learn enough to know how to defend those things in our Constitution that protect future generations of Americans.

Even when you agree with the idea that it's important to learn, and even when you try to do your best, there are many evil and negative forces that try to keep you from learning; they try to keep you from being an American hero. Some of these negative things are intentional to make you fail, others are accidental because some people don't understand success and happiness, or they don't care.

For example, some of your friends are jealous. If they see you learning and getting smart, they don't like it. They know you will soon know more than they do, or they will have to work harder to stay up with your level of being smart. Some people are too lazy to do that, or their families have not demonstrated the idea that education and learning are positive success things. Those families have learned to 'just get by.' They have no chance of ever being happy. Go on without them. It's your future.

Another problem is that our education system is confused with itself. A confused leader can never produce good leadership or a good positive plan. They do more harm than not even having a leader. For example, education leaders at the highest level have never even proclaimed the fundamental purpose for education. Without that recognition, they can never promote positive education. You must ignore this negative situation, and still try to learn. You can do it even without their help.

Finally, there are many who do not want you to learn enough to protect and defend our America. They want you to be a world student instead of a successful and proud American student. They do not want you to be an American hero or someone who worships God, our Creator. Surprise them. Prove that you still love our Blessed country: The United States of America, and that you still respect our Constitution.

About The Author

Will Clark's author experiences began by writing inspection and evaluation reports in the U.S. Air Force. He is a retired Air Force officer and a Vietnam veteran, serving in Saigon from 1966 to 1967. His other overseas assignments include Misawa, Japan and Ankara, Turkey. He taught on-base college courses while stationed in Turkey.

In 1995, as a 'Friends of Education' study skills project, he authored a book, *How to Learn*, to encourage students to improve their grades in DeSoto County, Mississippi. Education supporters printed and distributed four thousand copies. The following school year he wrote a weekly education column for a local newspaper, *The DeSoto County Tribune*. He also taught an adult GED class. His book, *How to Learn*, has been updated and is now available everywhere.

His next published book was *School Bells and Broken Tales*, a parody of nursery rhyme characters, also a motivation and education book for children. Other books include *Shades of Retribution,* a historical novel, and *Simply Success*, a motivation guide for students and employees.

His action novel, The Atlantis Crystal, is the first of a trilogy based on Atlantis and crystals. The other two books are: *She Waits in Atlantis*, and *Return to Atlantis*. This trilogy is based on his travels while assigned to Turkey, site of the ancient city of Troy. His latest political thriller is: *America 20XX: The New World Order.*

He is a past member of Toastmasters, a life member of Optimists International, a past Optimist Club president, and a past Optimist area lieutenant governor.

For more information about the author, visit:
AuthorsDen.com

Reading Opens Learning Doors

Other success books by the author

THE EDUCATION JUNGLE
How To Motivate, Educate, and Graduate
in The Education Jungle.

HOW TO LEARN
In Our Failed Education System

SIMPLY SUCCESS
The Student and Employee Handbook

THE PEER PRESSURE MONSTER
How to Recognize it And Avoid it

To learn more about the author and his books

Visit

AUTHORSDEN.COM

Reading Opens Learning Doors

www.ingramcontent.com/pod-product-compliance
Lightning Source LLC
Chambersburg PA
CBHW060153290526
45789CB00003B/1023